Troy Polamalu

by Mari Schuh

Consultant: Barry Wilner
AP Football Writer

BEARPORT
PUBLISHING

New York, New York

Credits

Cover and Title Page, © Gene J. Puskar/AP Images and Tom Hauck/AP Images; 4, © Keith Srakocic/AP Images; 5, © G. Newman Lowrance/AP Images; 6, © Gene J. Puskar/AP Images; 7, © Aaron Josefczyk/Icon SMI; 8, © Lisa Fletcher/iStockphoto; 9, © Daniel-life/Shutterstock Images; 10, © Zuma Press/Icon SMI; 11, © Icon SMI; 12, © Ted Timmons; 13, © Gary I. Rothstein/AP Images; 14, © Tom Hauck/Icon SMI; 15, © Daniel Hulshizer/AP Images; 16, © John Heller/AP Images; 17, © Icon SMI; 18, © Mark J. Terrill/AP Images; 19, © Mark Cowan/Icon SMI; 20, © Kevin Reece/Icon SMI; 21, © Zuma Press/Icon SMI.

Publisher: Kenn Goin
Editorial Director: Adam Siegel
Senior Editor: Joyce Tavolacci
Creative Director: Spencer Brinker
Photo Researcher: Arnold Ringstad
Design: Emily Love

Library of Congress Cataloging-in-Publication Data

Schuh, Mari.
   Troy Polamalu / by Mari Schuh.
      p. cm. — (Football stars up close)
   Includes bibliographical references and index.
   ISBN 978-1-61772-715-3 (library binding) — ISBN 1-61772-715-6 (library binding)
 1. Polamalu, Troy, 1981—Juvenile literature. 2. Football players—United States—Biography—Juvenile literature. I. Title.
   GV939.P65S34 2013
   796.332092—dc23
   [B]
                              2012037978

For more information, write to Bearport Publishing Company, Inc., 45 West 21st Street, Suite 3B, New York, New York 10010. Printed in the United States of America.

10 9 8 7 6 5 4 3 2 1

Contents

Big Play

It was the 2008 **playoffs**, and Troy Polamalu had to make a big play. His team, the Pittsburgh Steelers, was battling the Baltimore Ravens. Troy knew the winning team would go to the **Super Bowl**—and the Ravens now had a chance to score. If they could get the ball to the **end zone**, the Ravens would win the game. Could Troy stop them?

Troy rests at practice a few days before the big game against the Ravens.

Troy is on high alert before a play in the 2008 playoffs.

Troy is a safety, one of the players on the defense. A safety tries to keep players from the other team from catching passes and also makes **tackles**.

Super Bowl Bound

Troy watched Ravens player, Joe Flacco, throw the football. Troy ran toward the ball, reached high into the air, and **intercepted** the pass. He tucked the ball into his arms and ran as fast as he could. He twisted and turned past Ravens players, speeding into the end zone for a **touchdown**. Thanks to Troy, the Steelers won the game 23–14. They were on their way to the Super Bowl!

Troy (#43) moves to tackle a Cardinals player during the Super Bowl.

The 2009 Super Bowl was played in Tampa, Florida. The Pittsburgh Steelers defeated the Arizona Cardinals 27–23.

Troy dashes toward the end zone after intercepting Joe Flacco's pass.

California to Oregon

Troy was born on April 19, 1981, in Garden Grove, California. He and his family lived in a rough, crime-filled neighborhood. In 1989, his mother took him to visit his aunt and uncle in Tenmile, Oregon. Troy loved being in Oregon and asked his mom if he could live there. Troy's mom agreed that Oregon would be a safer place for her son to grow up. Soon after, Troy began his new life in Tenmile.

Troy's family comes from American Samoa, a group of islands in the South Pacific Ocean.

A beach on one of the islands of American Samoa

Troy liked fishing and camping in Oregon.

Young Athlete

Growing up in Oregon, Troy loved playing baseball and basketball. In the fifth grade, he started playing football in local leagues. Troy impressed his coaches by scoring a touchdown on one of his first plays ever. He was both fast and smart on the field. With Troy's help, the team became one of the best in the league.

Troy still wears contact lenses when he plays football.

One of Troy's fourth-grade baseball coaches noticed that he was having a tough time seeing the ball. He told Troy's aunt to take him to the eye doctor, where Troy got contact lenses.

Troy ran fast as
a child—and
runs even faster
as an adult.

High School Star

In 1995, Troy began attending Douglas High School in Winston, Oregon. He played football, basketball, and baseball. However, football was by far his favorite sport. His amazing speed and strength made him the best player on his high school team. When Troy was a senior, he tore a back muscle during a game. As a result, he sat out the rest of the 1998 season. That didn't stop colleges from asking this talented athlete to come to their school, however.

Douglas High School

Home of the "TROJANS"

Troy was also a great baseball player in high school. He played center field and was picked for Oregon's All-State team.

Troy talking with a coach from the University of Southern California

College Football

In 1998, Troy accepted a football **scholarship** to the University of Southern California (USC). Troy played as a **starter** on the USC team for three years. He thrilled fans with his fast footwork and power. During his junior year, he made an incredible 118 tackles. Game after game, Troy proved himself to be a rising star. Because of his amazing skills, Troy was named an **All-American player** in 2001 and 2002.

Troy stretches before a 2002 game.

In 2002, Troy was one of three finalists for the Jim Thorpe Award. This award is given to an outstanding defensive player in college football.

Troy (#43) runs for a touchdown during a college game.

Playing in Pittsburgh

After his spectacular college career, many **NFL** teams wanted Troy to play for them. The Pittsburgh Steelers chose him in the first round of the 2003 NFL **draft**. Troy quickly showed that the Steelers had made a great choice. He was strong enough to make tough tackles and quick enough to intercept many passes. Troy was on his way to becoming one of the top defensive players in the NFL.

The NFL draft is held every year. Troy was the first safety the Steelers had ever chosen during the first round of the draft.

Troy smiles after being drafted by the Steelers.

Troy intercepts a pass in a 2010 game against the Tennessee Titans.

Troy the Champion

Troy and his teammates worked hard on the field, and it paid off. In 2006, the Steelers beat the Seattle Seahawks 21–10 to win the Super Bowl. A few years later, Troy made an impressive seven interceptions during the season before going to the 2009 Super Bowl. There, the Steelers defeated the Arizona Cardinals 27–23.

Troy (#43) makes a tackle during the 2009 Super Bowl.

In blocking an Indianapolis Colts player during a 2006 game, Troy knocks him to the ground.

Between 2005 and 2012, Troy was picked seven times for the Pro Bowl. The Pro Bowl is the NFL's all-star game.

Fan Favorite

Off the field, Troy is soft-spoken and full of compassion for others. He and his wife created the Troy and Theodora Polamalu Foundation. The organization helps build homes for people in American Samoa. On the field, Troy is fearless. Fans love to watch him make tackles and dazzling interceptions. Thanks to his speed, strength, and skill, Troy has become one of the NFL's biggest stars.

Troy with his wife, Theodora, after a 2006 game

It's easy to spot Troy on the field. Just look for his long, black, curly hair. Troy's hair is so famous that he has even starred in shampoo commercials.

Troy practices before the 2012 season.

21

Troy's Life and Career

☆ **April 19, 1981** — Troy Polamalu is born in Garden Grove, California.

☆ **1989** — Troy moves to Tenmile, Oregon, to live with his aunt and uncle.

☆ **1998** — Troy is injured in a game during his senior year of high school.

☆ **1999** — Troy begins playing football for the University of Southern California.

☆ **2001** — Troy is named an All-American player.

☆ **2002** — Troy is named an All-American player for the second year in a row.

☆ **2003** — Troy is chosen by the Pittsburgh Steelers in the NFL draft.

☆ **2006** — The Steelers beat the Seattle Seahawks 21–10 in the Super Bowl.

☆ **2009** — The Steelers beat the Arizona Cardinals 27–23 in the Super Bowl.

☆ **2011** — The Steelers win in the playoffs but lose the Super Bowl 31–25 to the Green Bay Packers.

Glossary

All-American player
(AWL-uh-MER-uh-kuhn PLAY-ur)
a college player named as one of
the best in the country by sports
reporters

All-State team (AWL-STAYT TEEM)
a team made up of the best players
in the state

draft (DRAFT)
an event in which professional
football teams take turns choosing
college players to play for them

end zone (END ZOHN)
the area at either end of a football
field where touchdowns are scored

intercepted (in-tur-SEPT-ed)
caught a pass that was meant for
the other team

NFL (EN-EFF-ELL)
letters standing for the National
Football League, which includes
32 teams

playoffs (PLAY-awfss)
the games held after the end of
the regular football season that
determine which two teams will
compete in the Super Bowl

scholarship (SKOL-ur-ship)
money given to a student to attend
school

starter (STAR-tur)
a player who is the coach's first
choice to play in a game

Super Bowl (SOO-pur BOHL)
the final championship game in the
NFL season

tackles (TAK-uhlz)
plays in which a player grabs
players from the other team and
drags or knocks them to the ground

touchdown (TUHCH-*doun*)
a score of six points that is made
by getting the ball across the other
team's goal line

Index

Bibliography

Official Site of the Pittsburgh Steelers: www.steelers.com

Official Site of Troy Polamalu: www.troy43.com

Official Site of the USC Trojans: www.usctrojans.com

Read More

Polzer, Tim. *Defense!* New York: Scholastic (2011).

Sandler, Michael. *Troy Polamalu (Football Heroes Making a Difference).* New York: Bearport (2012).

Tracy, Kathleen. *Troy Polamalu (A Robbie Reader).* Hockessin, DE: Mitchell Lane (2012).

Learn More Online

To learn more about Troy Polamalu, visit
www.bearportpublishing.com/FootballStarsUpClose